Table of Contents

Definitions

A good place to first broach the concepts that we will be covering in this book is a list of definitions. It cannot be comprehensive because terms and use are in a very active state of flux. As people explore both their own concepts of gender identity as well as we, as a society, attempt to move beyond a binary definition of gender, we are all searching for a way forward and attempting to find the right path. We will have false starts and changes in direction. It will be ok.

Perhaps the most important concept in this entire book is really not that complicated. Just accept people for who they say they are and treat them with respect. It isn't too hard to imagine that we should trust that people know who they are or at least should be given the latitude to find themselves, and it's not ours or anyone else's place to tell them who they are. It's ok. Their identity is not an insult to you and your identity. You know you, they know them, I know me.

Transgender:

At this stage of the game, most of us understand what the word transgender means. It means that a person's identity today is different than the one assigned at birth. Many people further restrict it to mean that they are transitioning. That is an unnecessary limitation. If you identify as transgender, you are transgender. There are no prerequisites or criteria that are required to qualify for being transgender.

The specifics are far harder to define but we will attempt to explore the details throughout the book so in effect, the entire book is a definition of transgender. The word is an adjective that is not a required part of a description of gender identity. A transgender woman is a woman and can check woman or female on a form. They do not need the word transgender unless they choose to list it. The same, of course, applies for all other people and identities. Transgender is often used as an umbrella term to refer to all gender diverse people. Some people would prefer not to consider themselves transgender, though, as it assigns special significance to the gender assigned at birth, something we will cover in more detail in a little bit.

Gender Identity:

While the official definition is something along the lines of "a person's internal sense of being male or female," that definition is lacking both in its fixation on there only being two genders as well as a lack of inclusiveness of everyone. Dealing with the first portion of it, we have to remember that gender cannot be rigidly defined as male or female. We will spend time later exploring the concepts of non-binary genders, binary being one of two choices. For now, please just accept the concept that gender is on a spectrum like a dimmer switch, with every person having elements traditionally defined as male and traditionally defined as female. The second portion, the inclusiveness of everyone, means that everyone has a gender identity even if you never spent any time thinking about it.

Gender Diverse/ Gender Expansive/ Gender Creative:

These terms are in active flux. Some people prefer using one and some another. Still others use terms like gender non-binary or gender non-conforming. Please see the entries for the latter two separately.

All are an attempt to positively identify a group of people who identify outside of a gender binary. In this book, I advocate that the binary is false to begin with. While we as a society are used to thinking in terms of male and female, those identities are loosely defined when we begin to delve into what they mean. Please see the section on gender diversity.

I personally prefer the term gender diverse and will use it throughout the book. The difference is minimal. Over time, the community will settle on one term or the other, and I will happily adopt that.

Someone who identifies as gender diverse or non-binary feels that their gender identity falls outside of the idea of being either male or female. The list of gender identities is seemingly endless and growing every day. If someone tells you their gender, and it is a term you don't recognize, I suggest you offer your pronouns and ask for theirs. If it is important to you to understand what their gender is, then I suggest you google it later as the process of constantly educating people can make you feel like a walking Wikipedia entry.

This is often the most challenging concept for people who grew up before the internet to wrap their heads around. Americans are very excited to categorize and generalize. These generalizations help us follow cultural rules our parents taught us. Take, for example, the idea that men hold the door for women. If a man who prides himself on following this rule he was taught growing up goes through a door, he may be faced with a dilemma. If he looks back at the person following him through the door to determine if that person is a woman --so he knows whether to hold the door--but is unable to place that person in a category, it upsets a fundamental rule of his life that he is proud of his adherence to. In that circumstance, I would advise the man to not drop the door on whoever is following him but beyond that, do whatever he likes. Hold the door, hand off the door, whatever-- just let the need to classify go, because despite whatever frustration he may feel, the person behind him just wants to enter the building or room. If the lack of the ability to categorize someone is bothering you, look inside yourself to find the source of the problem rather than at the other person. They don't need to fit in a box for you.

Pronouns:

Most of us learned what a pronoun was in middle school English class. They play a special role when interacting with people of a diverse gender identity though. Just like you would not refer to your female friend with he, it is important that you use the proper pronoun when interacting with everyone. This is tantamount to an announcement that you respect them and their gender identity. Part of the importance is driven by the use of pronouns to insult transgender and gender diverse people. As a transgender woman, people will often use he/him when talking about me to designate my transgender status and specifically state that they don't accept my gender identity. It is also a form of aggression designed to ridicule or designate me as less than them. It in effect says there is something wrong with me because my gender identity does not match the gender assigned at my birth.

The most common pronouns are well known to all of us. He/him/his for male identified people, she/her/hers for female. Because you can't always tell, the proper procedure is to announce your pronouns as you ask for theirs. People who do not identify as male or female will most frequently use they/them/theirs. Despite what you may have been taught many years ago in school, it is grammatically correct to use these pronouns to refer to a single person. There are other pronouns that receive less frequent use but still are valid. Just use whatever people ask you to use. People make mistakes. Just apologize, correct yourself and move on. It is not required to make a big deal about it, but it is important that you make an effort. Like with any skill, switching between pronouns will take practice, but you will get better at it.

If you have known the person you are talking to for a long time, and they recently changed pronouns, it is important that you adapt. Just knowing them a long time does not release you from the obligation to treat them with respect. In my opinion, it does give you a special level of forgiveness when you repeatedly make mistakes but, because of your closeness, it is also especially important for you to validate their gender identity by using the correct pronouns as that closeness brings with it an increased level of hurt when you use the wrong pronouns or otherwise invalidate their gender identity.

Gender Assigned at Birth/Gender Designated at Birth:

It is not a surprise to anyone that when a baby is born, among the first words out of the doctor's mouth is "it's a boy" or "it's a girl." Many parents learn an assigned gender well before the birth either by ultrasound or genetic testing. Knowing the gender of a baby is part of the dreaming that all parents do about their upcoming family addition. All of the things they dream of doing together and the conversations they have with their friends and family so often revolve around the gender of the baby.

For most children, this is nothing more than a natural part of growing up in the twenty-first century. The doctor says boy or girl and they then grow to define the details themselves as they grow up and older.

For some children though, the result of the gender assignment and the cultural expectations that come with it is the first act of violence committed against them. By assigning the baby a gender, they are placed in a box. This box determines everything from what color their baby room is painted to how people describe them. Are they pretty or smart? Are they strong or sweet? Do they look like mom or dad? What name are they given? Are they put in a dress? How about a bow in their hair? All of these things begin to shape them and how they see the world. Even the language so often used to express positive feelings like "he is going to be a lady killer" or "she will have to beat the boys off with a stick" can, in the long term, undermine their self-confidence and vision of themselves if they are homosexual or transgender. As an aside, why is the violence in those terms let off as not really meaning anything?

Beyond the doctor's assignment and parental expectations, inscribing a gender on the birth certificate fixes in legal stone a portion of their identity before anyone has had a chance to ask them.

There is no question that each parent must, at these stages of life, make the decisions they think are best for their child. And furthermore, there is so much cultural pressure to conform to these norms that I think the most important course of action that parents can take is to pay attention to their children as they mature and allow them to find themselves and work hard to validate them at each stage of their lives.

There are some circumstances, however, when the parents must take charge and push back against doctors. This is in respect to children born with ambiguous genitalia.

Intersex:

The exact percentage of children born who are intersex is unclear but the numbers are as high as 1 in 250, although those specifically born with genitals that don't easily fall in to generally accepted norms of male or female are closer to 1 in 2000. The problem comes when doctors recommend taking some sort of corrective action. A poorly designed study led many years ago led to intersex children being routinely operated on, and then raised as a different gender. If your new baby is born with any sort of intersex trait, it is important that you consult actual experts before making decisions that will affect your child's entire life. The likelihood that your doctor is qualified to advise you is slightly more than zero, but the likelihood they will attempt to advise you is very high. Step back and think about these decisions. Like anything that will affect your child every day for the rest of their lives, it deserves some thought and research.

Other Definitions:

Cisgender:
A person's gender identity matches the gender they were assigned at birth. Just like the word transgender, it is an adjective that is optional in its use.

Clock/Read:
When a transgender person is identified by a stranger as being transgender, they often say they were clocked or read.

Coming Out:
This is the process of announcing your gender identity, sexual orientation, and any desires to transition to others. This is a big process that does not happen all at once. I have chosen to dedicate an entire section to it later in the book.

Dead Name:
Pre transition name… i.e. generally the name given at birth that has been left behind as a person transitions. Some but not all transgender people choose a new name more representative of their post transition self. The use of that name is called dead naming and is often used as a way to show disrespect and lack of acceptance of transgender and gender diverse people.

Guevedoces:
Guevedoces are members of a population in the Dominican Republic who, because of a genetic trait, are born and assigned female, but at age 12 they grow a penis. The literal translation is "penis at 12." This is one example of an intersex trait.

Gender Non-Binary:

Similar to the gender non-conforming, gender non-binary refers to a gender outside of the binary. It remains a common term, and you are likely to find people who use it regularly.

For the term gender non-binary to mean something, it requires that a binary gender exist and that is a false attempt at categorization. Therefore, gender diverse or gender expansive would generally be preferred terms but, do not correct someone if they describe themselves as non-binary. It is up to each of us to decide how we want to identify and how we describe that identity. Use whatever terminology they ask you to use. Each of us can never be wrong when describing ourselves.

Gender Non-Conforming:

This term is used as an alternative to gender diverse, but because of its suggestion that there is a gender to conform to and these people are outside of that norm, it is often considered a microaggression.

Gender Presentation/Gender Expression:

This is the way each person decides to portray themselves to the world. Do you wear dresses? Athletic jerseys and jeans? Do you wear makeup or have facial hair? Do you wear jewelry?

Lantinx:

Genderless version of Latino or Latina.

Mama Bear/Papa Bear:

These are terms adopted by the parents of LGBTQIA youth who have chosen to step out and advocate for, as well as protect, their children. Unbelievably, parents can face considerable criticism because they have chosen to be supportive of their LGBTQIA children. This is especially true for parents of transgender kids. These outstanding parents also need our support and allyship.

Microaggression:

A microaggression is language that chips away at self-confidence and is invalidating of people's gender identity or othering (defines people as different or abnormal) but is not overtly insulting. A classic example would be: "You look pretty for a trans woman." It is a compliment but, at the same time an insult. Other examples might be describing cisgender women as "real women." Microaggression's are also commonly heard by racial minorities. An example of that might be asking a lantinx or asian person "Where are they really from?"

Othering:

The use of words or phrases that define a person as outside of a group or a cohort.

Stealth:

Stelth is a term used when a person who has transitioned genders lives in their new gender without the people they interact with knowing they have transitioned.

Transiversary:

Exactly which date a transgender person uses to identify as their rebirth date varies somewhat, but it is often called their transiversary. Many people use the date they first started hormone replacement therapy. Others use the date they began transition or the date they realized they were transgender.

Transgender man:

A transgender man is a person whose gender assigned at birth is female but whose gender identity is male.

Transgender woman:

A transgender woman is a person whose gender assigne
birth is male but whose gender identity is female.

Transsexual:

Transsexual is a word that many people have moved away from
using, but it maintains importance for some people. It is a
specific medical term that describes someone who wishes to
complete a medical transition. Some consider it problematic
because it has a lot of emphasis on surgery, which is out of
reach for many people who are transgender because of cost,
availability, and other obstacles. Some states have used surgery
as a legal obstacle to completing transition and allowing
correction on birth certificates or other legal documents, and it
places the focus directly on the physical form rather than
gender identity. For those reasons and others, it has fallen out
of use by many, but it remains an important part of identity for
some.

Two Spirit:

Two spirit is a traditional Native American description of people
who do not fit within a binary gender definition. This concept
was common among North American indigenous people and
has existed for thousands of years.

Gender vs Sex

It is important to divide physiological condition from gender as the two are separate. Gender is in the mind while sex is the physical. This is hard for a lot of people to get their heads around because for most people, sex and gender are connected.

Just as challenging is the concept that neither sex nor gender are binary; one or the other. As there are more than two genders--more than man and woman--there are more than two sexes--male and female.

Gender diversity is broad and definitions are constantly becoming more inclusive with new articulated identities being defined all the time. Just seek out the gender identity options available to users of Tumblr for a brief window into the amazing diversity of gender. Hundreds of permutations are there for people to use to identify themselves.

Sexual diversity is similarly broad with different intersex conditions easy to read about. These range from chromosomal variation from XXY, XXX and XYY to various hormonal variation involving sensitivity to various hormones. It's important to realize that the grossly simplistic XX and XY/male and female that you were taught in elementary school science is not accurate and does not correctly represent the reality of sexual diversity.

Sexual Orientation vs Gender Identity

It is also very important to remember that who we are attracted to is not connected with our gender identity. The majority of the people who transition do not change who they are attracted to. If anything, exploration of gender identity may encourage them to challenge other assumptions taught to them but, for most, there is no change.

Transgender: The Science

I start this section on the science of being transgender by first stating that the mechanisms are not important. Trust that people know and can tell you how they feel and who they are. I cover the science only because firstly, poorly understood science is so often used to argue against people being transgender and secondly, because some transgender people feel validated if a little science was there to back them up.

Several studies have been done that validate the status of transgender people. I shall attempt to summarize a few of the studies.

Genetic basis for being transgender

Several studies have looked at identical twins vs fraternal twins and found that more often than not, identical twins who, because they are identical, have identical genetic makeup, are more often both transgender than fraternal twins who, because they are fraternal, do not share the same genetic makeup. The scientific community often sees these studies as evidence that genetics plays a role.

Looking in the brain

Several additional studies have examined various structures in the brain and compared them between cisgender people and transgender people. The methodologies were different, but the outcomes were the same. In each of the studies, the brains of the transgender women much more closely matched the brains of the cisgender women and the brains of the transgender men more closely matched the brains of the cisgender men. Just because this is often a follow-up question, the brains of cisgender gay men matched the brains of cisgender heterosexual men. These results were consistent both before and after hormone replacement therapy.

Theories

There are several theories as to what causes people to be transgender, and there may not be a single cause. Most have to do with hormones during early developmental stages in the womb. Exposure to heightened levels of testosterone or estrogen or different sensitivity to these hormones during critical points in development are the most common prominent theory.

There are also some theories based on epigenetics, but most of these are outside the scope of this book.

In the 50s and 60s, a drug abbreviated as DES was often given to women to help with morning sickness. The drug is a synthetic estrogen and a few studies have found a connection showing an increased likelihood of being transgender among children born to women who received the drug.

In the end and just to reiterate, trust what people tell you about themselves. The why is less important.

Transition

The process of transitioning your gender is a unique process and experience for each person. No transition is the same as any other. There is no roadmap that defines the steps that need to be taken nor what the end goal looks like. Each person's gender identity is unique as are their motivations, resources, circumstances, etc..

Typically, the process of transition is divided in to three parts: social transition, legal transition and medical transition.

Social Transition

Social transition is defined as the process of changing your gender presentation. Like gender identity, each person has a different way they want people to perceive them and a different way they want to dress that makes them feel happy with themselves. For a variety of reasons, gender identity may not line up with gender presentation.

When I transitioned at the office, I made an announcement to my supervisor and management that I planned to transition several months before I began wearing dresses and makeup. Furthermore, almost two years prior to telling my management I planned to transition, I knew my gender identity was female. During all that time, my gender identity remained female but my gender presentation in most of my life was male. These discrepancies happen for many reasons. For me, much of the time was my exploration of who I was and how I wanted to present myself and how to achieve those goals.

Also, I needed to figure out details about how my life would be effected post transition. How was my office going to respond? What policies were in place at work to protect me? What about legal protections? How was my family going to respond? Just answering all these questions for some people take years. For all of that time, their gender identity remains hidden behind their gender expression. There are many consequences to social transition. Among the most significant is the loss of invisibility. When most people enter a room, people glance at them and classify them neatly into some category. This is not always positive, especially with members of marginalized communities. This loss of invisibility can be especially challenging for white people who spent a long time presenting as male whose presence carried with them significant privilege. The sudden loss of that privilege is an eye-opener for many. Privilege is invisible and a hard pill to swallow. Many a transgender woman has been trapped in her house unable to leave while expressing their true identity out of fear of being seen and becoming the object of ridicule and discrimination. The gaining of privilege is also among the most commonly remarked upon experiences of transgender men who suddenly gain male privilege after they transition.

Among the first pieces of advice received by people wishing to transition is to pick someone to emulate as they start to make decisions. As a transgender woman, I was given by advice sites online a number of movie and television characters. I chose Holly GoLlghtly from *Breakfast at Tiffany's*. This persona and look is just a starting place from which you build your personal look and presentation. I like dressing nicely. I am a big fan of dresses and jewelry and a very obviously feminine look. My desire to look feminine is so strong that when I choose a more casual even marginally androgynous look I find it triggering, and I begin to obsess with greater and greater urgency. Just a graphic t-shirt and jeans is enough to drive me to neurotically obsess over my hair and other portions of my look. Despite the obvious convenience and commonality of that look, I have found that I am better off seeking dresses and choosing outfits that verge on too dressy for the occasion. I have found that my vision of myself and the way I think people see me is often very wrapped up in the clothing. I want them to take me seriously, and I want them to take my female presentation seriously, so I want it to be clear that I gave thought and invested energy in presenting a specific look. Ironically that seems to deviate from the character Holly Golightly who just seemed to fall into a very feminine presentation.

As an ally, be sure to allow the transgender and gender diverse people in your life to find their path. Being ready to offer advice is good but, as with all advice, is not always wanted. For me, having my wife invite me to get a pedicure and share in that experience was so valuable. It validated my identity and allowed me to share in an experience that is often shared between women. Very often, this easy step is intensely appreciated. I know it was for me.

Legal Transition

Legal transition is the process of making your legal documentation match your gender identity. This is a complicated process that changes depending on where you live. Each state in the US has different laws, and in some states a complete legal transition is impossible. The lack of legal documentation can make even mundane interaction with government representatives and others unnecessarily complicated. Imagine getting pulled over by police and presenting them with a male ID while wearing makeup and a dress. If you have seen people go through transition, you have seen firsthand how dramatically their look has changed. A photo ID showing a transgender person prior to transition is not very effective.

Most government agencies in the United States require some sort of medical certification that you are transitioning. At the time of this writing, for an updated passport or social security card, a letter from a medical doctor will be required certifying that the person has received appropriate medical treatment to transition genders. The specific wording is available online.

While each doctor is different, many require a certification by a therapist that medical treatment is appropriate. Many therapists require as much as a year of therapy before being willing to make that determination.

In effect, the therapists and the medical doctors are gatekeepers of the ability for a transgender person to begin transition.

For most states, to update your gender marker on your birth certificate, a court order will be required. Often, letters from both a therapist and an MD are required for that to take place and, in many states, judges routinely deny gender marker change.

Of course, the process for a name change is well established and generally presents less confusion, although, there are many stories of judges being unwilling to change a name because it is a woman's name and the gender marker says male or vice versa.

When I appeared in court, I was all prepared to defend my gender marker change. I had chosen a judge from a list of judges online that were friendly to the process, and I had the benefit of a lawyer friend who was walking me and two others through the court system that day. I sat patiently in court waiting for my name to be called and rehearsing the answers to any questions from the judge in my head.

When my name was called and I approached the bench, the judge asked a few questions and then asked about where I was born. My mind sprang into action and filtered through my prepared answers getting them ready for the confrontation. I answered Minnesota, assuming he was wondering why I had not checked the box asking for a changed birth certificate. All my preparation was tossed out the window as the Judge launched into a discussion about being from Waco, Texas, and knowing other people with my last name.

My lawyer friend explained to me later that judges who sit in these courts spend much of their days making people unhappy. They are ruling on divorces or on small claims or whatever. When a name and gender maker change come through, they often just want to have a pleasant conversation with someone who they are making so very happy.

All the doctors' visits, notary and other court costs, and various fees often make a legal transition very expensive on top of the time and effort needed to jump through all the hoops. Costs can range from the hundreds into several thousands, if legal representation is required.

From the perspective of being an ally, understanding that legal name and gender marker change are often very complicated and expensive is important. The seemingly simple requirement of demanding a legal ID can make it impossible for gender diverse people to participate. If that cannot be avoided, making provisions for the use of a preferred name and for recording and using the proper pronouns can help make your program more inclusive. Be sure to train your staff on how to appropriately manage these circumstances. Confused staff making a big deal and outing gender diverse people can be uncomfortable or even dangerous for the transitioning person.

Medical Transition

Medical transition consists of the medical processes to transition genders. As stated previously, the process is different for each person. No two people have the same desires or opportunities. Not everyone wants surgery or hormones. Each person responds to hormones differently because of age and a long list of other biological reasons.

Trans feminine people often require a testosterone blocker and estrogen or sometimes may go on estrogen and progesterone. The hormones will make skin softer and more sensitive and body hair finer. Fat will deposit in the hips, butt, and chest and away from the midsection. Facial features will also often become softer in appearance. Typically, cholesterol levels and blood pressure will also drop.

Trans masculine people will often go on testosterone. This will trigger muscle growth and fat will more commonly deposit around the midsection. Often cholesterol levels and blood pressure will increase.

Surgeries are very expensive and seldom covered by insurance. Breast removal or augmentation is often as much as $10,000 and bottom surgery can rapidly exceed $40,000. There is also often bed rest associated with these procedures, making extended time away work yet another hurdle to overcome. It is not uncommon for people wanting surgery to go to Thailand or Mexico to mitigate costs.

Trans feminine people will often want hair removal. Despite being the least expensive among the medical interventions, it is common to spend $20,000 just having hair removed.

Laser hair removal, especially on the face, takes many treatments--depending on the laser type and color of skin and hair. The best candidates are fair-skinned people with dark hair. Lasers utilize contrast to heat up the hair follicles and kill them at the root. It typically feels like a rubber band being snapped on your face and it requires 30-40 zaps on a typical face. Larger areas of the body obviously require more zaps with the laser. Facial hair is the most stubborn.

Even after a face has been considered cleared of hair, often periodic treatments will be required to keep it that way.

Electrolysis is the only actual permanent hair removal technique. Because it is expensive, often around $120 per hour per technician, often people start with laser and switch to electrolysis for clean-up. There are places that will numb the whole face, and then using two technicians, will clear the entire face. This process will often take eight hours and the face is left bruised and swollen.

Because all hair does not grow at the same time, completely clearing an area of hair does not mean more hair won't show up later. Often, new hair grows in that is different from the hair that was removed.

Some, when they are unable to find qualified medical care or are unwilling to out themselves in order to receive care, attempt to transition on their own. Drugs and protocols are readily available, but potential consequences are high. While hormones are generally believed to be safe, the effect of manipulating hormones without testing to make sure proper levels are achieved and maintained can be very dangerous and lead to blood clots or other potentially fatal side effects.

The most common way that people transition on their own is to obtain birth control pills from a sister or a girlfriend. Other means are to order pills or estrogen creams off the internet. While stories of success exist, results are inconsistent and unpredictable.

People who are determined to transition on their own are not likely to be deterred by discussions of safety or inconsistent results. This advice is common online. The best you can do to support them is try to find them the appropriate care and make sure they know how to access it and have the resources to do so.

Similar challenges exist for quality psychological care. Often trained therapists are hard or impossible to find. To be clear, not every person transitioning needs psychological care. When they do need care, they need someone who has received training associated with gender identity. It's not that the care is really all that different, but having a therapist familiar with concepts is valuable and often the therapist will be asked to provide letters supporting further medical care. It's important not to invest time and money into a therapist that will be unable to fulfill these requirements.

Coming Out

The coming out process for people who are transgender is often very different than that for people who are gay or lesbian. If they chose to, it is possible for a lesbian or a gay person to move through a space with their sexuality invisible, i.e., nobody would know they are homosexual. But for many people who are transgender, the process of transitioning in itself sometimes makes them visible as soon as they enter a room. For others, an incomplete legal transition forces them to announce their gender transition during interactions with government bodies. In most cases, just purchasing an item can out them as their name on their credit card or driver's license does not match their gender presentation.

Many people have experienced coming out. Perhaps, they were on a on a diet of some kind. You plan to go out to eat with friends, and you must announce your diet and have that influence the plans of the group. It is sometimes tinged with guilt as you force a change of restaurants. You may be greeted with words of encouragement or unwanted advice. Perhaps it will be suggested that this is the wrong diet for you or perhaps you should just eat in advance or not join them for this evening out.

Coming out about being transgender is, as I suggested, different though. Often, people can see you are transgender. You can hide your diet. Once you have been transitioning for a while, mannerisms, breast growth or hair growth may make your transition obvious. While most people can understand being on a diet and have been on one themselves, few people understand what it is like to be assigned the wrong gender at birth and to go through the process of transitioning. They may have opinions about it formed from incomplete or incorrect information. Often, they have heard a church sermon condemning you or heard political leaders speak out against you. Talking heads on TV screens debate your mental sanity or advocate exclusion from the public presence by denying your access to public facilities. They equate you with pedophiles. Others, so anxious to compensate for the horrible responses they know you receive, work so hard at being supportive that it gets awkward and makes everyone uncomfortable.

Most transgender and gender diverse people just want to live their lives. They don't want to talk about their transgender status and educate everyone they meet. They just want to go through their daily activities without hassle or obstacle like everyone else. A pleasant smile and polite interaction is all that is required.

If a close friend comes out to you. Make it clear that this will have no effect on their relationship to you. Share your pronouns and ask for theirs and if you like, ask them what kind of help or support they need.

Understand that you may have known the person for a very long time and for all that time, they may not have come out to you. There are a lot of reasons for this. Perhaps they were not in the process of transitioning but that has now changed or perhaps they did not know how you would react.

Many transgender and gender diverse people lose everything when they transition. Their families, friends, children, jobs, club memberships, and many other important things can be lost. For that reason, many choose just to continue to hide their true identity, thinking life is not worth living without all they believe would be lost.

As you can imagine, it's very hard to turn back once you begin down that path. People know you have started to transition, and that in itself is pressure. Once people know, it effects how they interact with you and decisions they make in regard to you.

Kristin Beck, subject of the CNN Documentary *Lady Valor* describes an alternate version of coming out. She instead uses the metaphor of a great room. She describes coming out as being a concept of our parents. Coming out, which is short for coming out of the closet, is an all-or-nothing prospect, she says. You are out or you are not out. She lived for many years as a Navy SEAL, where she could not share her identity openly. To her, instead of being in the closet, which is dark and horrible, you are instead in a great room with a big screen TV and comfortable furniture. As time goes on, you invite others into your great room to share in this portion of your life. As you do so, the room gets bigger and the party more fun.

Every time a person is required to come out, the response they receive is based in how coming out effects the lives of the person they are coming out to. For example, if someone comes out to a parent and that parent is deeply involved in a church that is not affirming of gender diversity, the parent may push back out of fear about how their relationship with the church may be effected. Often as those fears are settled, the resistance declines.

Whatever the coming out process is for the transgender people in your life, trust them to make the decisions they make at the time they make them. They must be in control of the process.

Do Not Out Anyone - EVER

The process of sharing someone's transgender status with others is called outing them and it is an act of violence. Because of the potential discrimination and the potentially far reaching consequences of people learning someone is transgender, the transgender or gender diverse person must oversee all aspects of their out status. Do not under any circumstances share information shared with you. Treat it as a confidence of the utmost importance.

If you make a mistake, you must share it with the transgender person so they can decide what action to take. They need to know so they are not blindsided and can take whatever appropriate action they feel they need to manage the consequences.

If this happens, apologize and move beyond the error. Mistakes happen.

For me at this stage of my life and transition process, I am very out and so I am not careful who I come out to. I come out to most everyone, but it is still important to me that I am in control of the process because there may be specific circumstances when it can cause unnecessary complications.

This comes back to the proper use of name and pronouns. Using a person's dead name or incorrect pronouns in a public place creates an incongruity between how I present and how I am referred to that people usually pick up on. In effect, referring to me as "he" in a restaurant causes the waiter and people at tables near us to look at me and gender me. While it usually doesn't cause a problem, the prospect is there, especially in these politically charged times. I personally realize that for people I have known for dozens of years, there are mental pathways that have been established that must be given time to change, but, as you can see from the examples above, the potential consequences are real and serious.

Make a real effort to use the proper name and pronouns, and if you make a mistake, don't make a big deal about it because that just increases the likelihood that others will pick up on it. A simple apology and use of the proper name or pronoun is enough.

Were there ever really two genders?

What does it mean to be a man in the United States of America? That is really the question that most people obsess over as it has become easier and easier for women to defy gender stereotypes. Men are increasingly forced to live within a tighter and tighter set of rules. These rules often grow out of homophobia or the fear that heterosexual men will be perceived as homosexual. The rules are imposed at a young age, often to try to make sure that male children do not "turn out gay."

As I have stated before, everyone has a gender identity. For most people, it corresponds to the gender they were assigned at birth, but everyone has one.

Take a moment and think about your gender identity. If someone asked you your gender, what would you tell them?

Now, take another moment and ask yourself what it means to be that gender? How do you define being the gender you are?

As you define your gender, try not to do it by describing what you are not, e.g., you are a man because you are not a woman. Furthermore, you can't define your gender based on physical characteristics. There are people of different genders who also have those same characteristics, e.g., women with broad shoulders, men with breasts, or women who cannot carry a child.

As you define what it means to be your gender and recognize that some of those traits are also claimed by people who claim to be a different gender, ask yourself where the boundary is between genders.

If gender is on a spectrum, where along that spectrum does a man cease to be a man and a woman cease to be a woman?

The point here is that each of us must define for ourselves how we identify and what that means. A person who identifies as a man must define for himself what that is and what those boundaries are. It is not for anyone else to say whether decisions he makes about himself or his gender expression fit within the boundaries of a man. If this man identifies as gay, he must also define for himself what attracts him to a partner. It is not his job to police others identity or expression. It is only his job to decide if that identity or expression fits within the boundaries to which he is attracted.

The same criteria apply to all identities and all relationships.

Levels of acceptance

When you think of the transgender or gender diverse people in your life, what word do you use when you describe your feelings towards them?

I often hear people say they support transgender and gender diverse people. What do they mean when they say that? What do you mean when you say that? What are the limits of your support for the transgender and gender diverse people in your life? How public or private is your support? Does your support extend into voting to support their safety and human rights? Is your support limited to support for the transgender or gender diverse person you know or does it extend to all transgender and gender diverse people?

Read through these lists. Think about where your support stops and ask yourself why that is the case. No one is monitoring you. Be honest with yourself.

Each item is ranked from 1 being hostile to the highest number most supportive.

Private Support
1. I am actively trying to get them to deny their identity.
2. Their actions do not affect me; what they do is not my problem.
3. I am happy they are happy.
4. I love them and want to make them feel good about themselves.
5. I work with them to help them find ways to assist with their transition.

Public Support
1. If I hear family speak negatively about them, I will challenge that negativity.
2. If I hear friends speak negatively, I will challenge it.

3. If I hear anyone speak negatively, I will challenge it.
4. I will march or demonstrate my support publicly.

Political
1. I vote how I vote, how it affects them is not relevant.
2. I don't vote.
3. If I can use my vote to support them without changing parties or voting against something I care about, then I will.
4. I will contact my representative and ask them to vote to support them.
5. I will vote to support transgender and non-binary rights despite whatever my self-interest is.

Professional Support
1. I wouldn't want to speak up at work.
2. I will speak up at work.
3. I would work to create policies that support my transgender friend.
4. I would not enforce rules that discriminate if I could get away with it.
5. I refuse to enforce any discriminatory rules.

Philanthropic Support
1. I don't give money.
2. I will give to my church/organization but trust them to make good decisions.
3. I will give to my church/organization but take an interest in how they spend.
4. I refuse to give to organizations that do not support transgender/non-binary people.
5. I give to organizations that support transgender/non-binary rights.
6. I give to organizations that specifically serve transgender/non-binary people.

Religious organizations

1. What my church says, goes.
2. I do not like what my church says but would not speak up.
3. I speak up and challenge church discrimination.
4. I work with my church to reach out to transgender/gender diverse people.

Religious views

1. Transgender/gender diverse people will suffer the consequences of their decisions.
2. Everyone deserves access to religion, and they can change their ways to avoid consequences.
3. Religion has nothing to say about transgender and gender diverse people.
4. Religion is supporting of everyone and does not condemn.

Medical Acceptance

For many years, the psychological community had diagnosed people whose gender did not match the gender assigned at birth as having gender identity disorder. However, in recent years, they have come to understand that the problems and challenges they saw in transgender and gender diverse people were not the result of the incongruence in their gender identity vs the gender designated at birth. Instead they came to recognize that the real problem was in how friends, family, and society treated them. Furthermore, as gender diverse people received treatment, they found dramatic improvement in their psychological state and in very few cases, was there any regret, despite the significant effort put forth.

Meanwhile, medical doctors saw transgender patients responding to treatments that helped their bodies conform to their stated gender identity, so these treatments became the standard of care.

Meanwhile, medical researchers began to find some physiological evidence that supported the conclusions being formed by the doctors and the psychology community. Several very different studies compared portions of brains with cis-women, gay men, and transgender men and women and found that the brains of transgender women were much more similar to cis-women and the brains of gay men were much more similar to brains of heterosexual men and transgender men.

The result of this convergence is broad acceptance by medical associations, all of whom have published positions supporting the treatment of transgender and gender diverse people. Leading hospitals like the Mayo Clinic now offer treatments designed to support gender diverse people in their quest to have their physical body match their gender identity.

Of course, there remain hold outs--doctors who have made their careers appearing on TV or in court or writing literature that supports the gender binary. They do so despite the ever-growing mountain of evidence against their positions.

Sometimes transgender or gender diverse people seek validation of their feelings by wanting to have something to point to. Other times, others in society are looking for something that can be treated so the "problem" can be "fixed." It is important that the best measurement of transgender status or/and gender diversity is to ask the person involved. Believe them. There is nothing to be cured beyond providing them with the treatment that they say they require.

Therapists

Conversations I have had with therapists who are trained in supporting people whose gender is different than what was assigned at birth suggest that while the skills required to treat transgender and gender diverse people are the same as other treatment, it's better if the therapists have had some training, and better yet, some experience working with transgender people. Ignorance can be damaging. Additionally, the therapist will likely be eventually asked to provide a letter either for gender marker change or medical treatment. Before investing time in a therapist, make sure the therapist knows this is or could be the goal. If they are unwilling to provide that letter, seek out other care, if possible.

Medical Offices

A visit to the doctor is fraught with endless challenges ranging from ignorant or openly hostile medical staff to insurance problems to just sitting in the waiting room. While the American Medical Association as well as all other major medical associations have public statements supporting transgender people, as with all large groups, there are invariably people who either don't know, don't understand, or disagree.

In larger cities, you can seek out medical offices that specialize in care of transgender and gender diverse clients. In addition, at the time of this writing, Planned Parenthood was rolling out transgender services around the country as locations got trained.

A transgender person does not have the luxury of leaving details up to others. They must take control of their care. They must know where their insurance coverage stands and specifically what is covered.

Tests like PSA tests or pap smears will often initially be turned down if a legal gender marker change has been completed and will require follow-up.

Call ahead to talk to staff, if possible, so that they are not going in cold and they know what to expect.

It is also important to know the status of local emergency room care. Transgender patients with broken limbs have been turned away from facilities because of their transgender status even though obviously they need treatment.

I feel confident in saying that circumstances are improving, especially in US cities, and there are caring and educated physicians across America. Seek them out.

Bathrooms

Unfortunately, this book would not be complete without a discussion about bathrooms. The latest fashion among some groups has been to try to scare people into discriminating against transgender and gender diverse people by talking about bathroom predators. They talk about men in women's restrooms as if this were a thing even happening and use that talk to justify laws discriminating against the entire LGBTQIA community by overturning local ordinances designed to protect people from discrimination. These laws are required because local protections are far more effective than federal protections because of the cost and ease of. We all know that our personal direct interaction with the federal government is quite limited where our interactions with local governments is far more common. As an example, local governments enforce building codes. Some cities have passed ordinances stating that all single use restrooms must be open to all genders (gender neutral). Obviously, this is the same as the bathroom in your home. By declaring all single-use restrooms genderless, it solves a long list of challenges facing transgender and especially gender diverse people whose presentation is often outside of traditionally male or female. A visit to your local coffee shop is enough to demonstrate the dramatic increase in the number of safe restroom options brought about by these ordinances. Start to watch and you will begin to see single-use restrooms all over the place.

Especially early in my transition, I remember walking past several multi-use restrooms just to get to a coffee shop that I knew had a single-use restroom. The thought of standing in line and waiting to use the stalls in a ladies' room was unbearable. I was certain someone would question my presence, and because at the time my legal transition was not complete, I had nothing but my say-so as to why I was allowed in there.

Often, politicians and commentators quote safety as the reason for these laws. If any time is spent exploring this reasoning, though, it falls apart and, in fact, works directly in contrast to safety concerns.

First, most assaults of women do not occur in public restrooms. The clear majority occur at home by someone they know.

Second, in every case of ordinances that are passed designed to protect people's use of restrooms based on gender identity, laws against assault, voyeurism, photography and everything else that they espouse to be afraid of remain in effect. Furthermore, interviews of police in places where these laws have existed for dozens of years report no increase in these problems nor any other legal challenges.

Third, the laws usually talk about the use of birth certificates to verify gender. How many of us carry our birth certificates with us and are prepared to present them upon request whenever we use a public restroom? How many of us want to need to do this? It is possible for many transgender people to change the gender marker on their birth certificate but because of complexity, expense, and a general lack of need, only around 15% have done so. In addition, if they are not transitioning to male or female then very few places have any other option. Intersex people are particularly challenged in this instance and these laws would seem to need to allow designation of intersex on birth certificates. Only a few states and only a few times has this happened.

Fourth, the people really at risk of assault in restrooms are transgender and gender diverse people. 59% of transgender people report some sort of assault in public restrooms. Flexibility to use of the restroom that best matches gender presentation and where the transgender person feels safest is the best option.

Fifth, the laws really focus on the use of women's restrooms by people assigned male at birth. It is based on a false assumption that these people can be identified by looking at them. A quick google search for transgender women shows that they cannot be easily identified. Historically, the people most often confronted in ladies' rooms as a result of these laws are people assigned female at birth who may not present very feminine. Maybe they are in work-out clothing, maybe they have a disease like polycystic ovarian disease that causes them to appear more masculine, or maybe they just were just needing to run to the store and pick up some groceries and didn't have time to get all dressed up. Whatever the reasoning, few of us would consider laws that require women to put on makeup or a dress reasonable.

The laws also conveniently forget that people who were assigned female at birth who have transitioned to male would also be forced into the ladies' room.   Since the rise of these laws, many transgender men have courageously posted photos of themselves in ladies' rooms and they look as out of place as any man would. The real consequence is that by attempting to dictate bathroom use by the gender assigned at birth, we will end up with a circumstance that makes it impossible to determine who should be in the restroom.   Imagine walking in to a ladies' room and seeing a bearded, muscular person in there.   Would you feel the need to ask them to see their birth certificate? Would they have it? What if they didn't?

Sixth, what about applying this in our schools? Some schools have suggested that transgender children run across the school or campus to use the single-use restroom in the nurse's office. The extra time and effort to accomplish that poses challenges to students already under extra stress.   Interviews of these kids show that they end up avoiding eating and drinking in order to avoid bathroom use. Meanwhile when students are supported in their transition, few, if any, problems are ever reported. However, if the students do not receive support but instead are challenged by their school administration, other students often see this as license and even a message that transgender students are unacceptable and will respond with bullying.

Locker Rooms

As the bathroom arguments fall apart, often focus changes to the locker rooms. Older people think of community showers and imagine students with different genitals showering together. Most schools now, though, do not look like that. Instead, as people have desired greater privacy, most new locker rooms have showers segregated by walls, doors and curtains. People who are self-conscious about their body image can choose to change in the segregated spaces. The real solution here is to provide privacy to all rather than to focus on isolating transgender people.

Coming out at work

Transitioning at the office can be very stressful for transgender people. Legal protections are uneven and often unenforced. Furthermore, few employers list transition as a reason for terminating employment, making it hard to fight back against a termination.

Allies can assist by looking up local and state ordinances providing protection based on gender identity and sexual orientation as well as restroom use. Because most enforcement happens at the city or county level, those protections are the most effective and easiest to access.

Allies can also look to see if the company is ranked in the Human Rights Campaign's Corporate Index. This ranking is used to measure LGBTQIA inclusion and inclusive practices.

Also allies can look to see if gender identity is listed in a non-discrimination policy.

Help transgender people try to anticipate management concerns and other issues at the office and offer solutions when possible. That is not to say that all concerns are legitimate and they need to bend over backwards but, forward thinking demonstrates leadership. The outside perspective of an ally may be valuable in helping the transgender person develop a strategy.

Encourage the transgender person to communicate effectively. Unless there are other transgender or gender diverse people at the office, writing a letter to announce the decision to transition allows for management to adapt and become educated before they respond.

In the letter, they should specify what they want and what work will look like post-transition. Some items that may belong in the letter are:

- I will come to work conforming to the xxx dress code.
- I will use xxx rest rooms.
- Please address me using xxx name and xxx pronouns.

It is also valuable to provide a list of resources management can reference.

Elements of a supportive workplace

From a management perspective, it is most important that it be clear that the transitioning employee has the support of company management. This could be as simple as an announcement of the name change, new business cards, or perhaps a name tag, if those are in use. Some corporations will schedule training for employees. Still others will have a whole roll-out organized.

Many corporations have a defined process for transitioning. The Human Rights Campaign offers the following guidance for workplace transitions:

- Treat transgender employees in a manner consistent with their gender expression, including the use of appropriate names and pronouns

- Maintain confidentiality and privacy

- Provide training for coworkers and managers

- Demonstrate support at the highest levels of management

- Apply the same performance standards to transgender employees as to all other coworkers

- Enforce zero tolerance for harassment

- Create an employee resource group for transgender employees

- Include transgender employees in the organization's diversity metrics

In addition, look at the health plan offered to employees and include transition medical care if possible. Very often, because of the low number of transitioning employees, the costs are nominal across the insurance pool. This can make an incredible difference for transitioning employees.

College

Some students decide to wait to begin their exploration or transition until they leave for college. There could be many reasons for this ranging from concern of lack of support or disappointing family and friends to outright fear about the response. Other students are just unsure and are waiting until college to figure it all out.

Campus Pride ranks universities for LGBTQIA inclusion and supporting practices. They provide specific details for their rankings. This is a good place to start when considering a college or university.

Also, look online for non-discrimination statements. Most universities have one. Look for gender identity to be specifically listed.

Search through the student organizations and look for organizations that are dedicated to transgender and gender diverse people. If those do not exist, look to other LGBTQIA organizations.

Many universities also support a preferred name that will show up on class rosters and in other systems around campus. This can limit unintentional outing by university faculty and staff.

If restroom use is a concern, look for campus maps that show locations of all-gender or gender-neutral restrooms.

Housing is often a concern. If there is no way to specify housing placement preferences associated with being transgender or gender diverse, they may need to speak directly to housing staff to find accommodations.

Seek out diversity staff for assistance. They can usually help trans and gender diverse students navigate the bureaucracy of a college or university.

Intersectionality

Never are people just transgender or gender diverse. There are always other portions of their identities that intersect and create different challenges. Different religions, different economic circumstances, different cultural and racial backgrounds as well as so many other things all interact to create special circumstances, challenges, and opportunities.

Think in terms of your identity. How do you define who you are in the world? How do you define your gender? What is your skin color? How would your life have been different if your skin color was different? What about your access to education? What if the neighborhood you lived in had a poorly rated and underfunded school? Or, conversely, what if your neighborhood had a top-rated school with access to current technology and a comprehensive library? How did your skin color or your gender identity play into that access to education?

Based on study after study, we know that cultural expectations of girls play into their lack of interest in science and math. As early as elementary school, girls learn to focus away from STEM and instead focus on other things.

If your parents went to college, we know that you are more likely to attend college. We know that college degrees improve access to good paying jobs, gain access to health care and a seemingly endless list of other benefits.

Just a few generations ago, people of color were denied access to college. They were denied access to many schools. If your parents or grandparents had been uniformly denied access to education because of the color of your skin, we can start to see how the history of discrimination based on skin color plays into the marginalization of people.

The point here is that these factors add together to make up a person. They work together to define privilege and marginalization and opportunity.

These reasons are why transgender women of color are among the most marginalized identities in America today. In addition to being a person of color and a woman, they are also transgender. Not always, but far too often, they are left without access to a job, to housing, to family, to community. They are left without support structures that far too many of us take for granted and are left to try to survive. Far too many don't make it.

Trans Exclusionary Radical Feminism

There is a subset of feminist thinkers who rather than including women together based on shared experience, instead seek to exclude people from the moniker of womanhood. They try to lump transgender women in with cisgender men as if they had experienced male privilege the same as a cisgender man before they transitioned. Examination of the experiences of transgender women quickly shows that is not the case. The point of intersectionality as discussed above is that there is not a singular experience of being a woman. The experience of a white suburban woman in America is very different than a woman of color or other women around the world. Gendered spaces exist to provide brave spaces that allow people who have self-identified as that gender to grow and raise up both themselves and the others in that space.

Identifying gendered spaces

I attended a queer women's leadership conference and there was a question early on if the conference was open to feminine identified people outside the gender binary. The best way I have seen inclusive spaces used the words self-identified in front of the gender allowing people to decide if they fit in the space. i.e. The queer women's leadership is a conference for self-identified women to learn leadership skills and network with other self-identified women.

HIV/STD

There is nothing intrinsic about being transgender or gender diverse that increases the likelihood of HIV or STD infection but, because of abandonment, violence, or lack of access to resources, some transgender and gender diverse people may end up at higher risk than the general population.

Like everyone, they should always practice safe sex if they are sexually active. Condoms can make a difference. In addition, there are prophylactic medicines that further reduce the incidence of HIV infection. PREP is the name of one of these medicines. They should consult their doctor.

Free HIV and STD testing is commonly available in cities. Everyone, regardless of gender identity status should avail themselves of these services if they are sexually active. One reason for transgender people to get tested is because often these services are supported via grants and must test a minimum number of people to justify the grant. This free testing is valuable to the community as a whole both because the free testing is important for at risk people as well as accurate statistics of HIV infection in the transgender and gender diverse community are hard to come by. The result is a lack of money and resources devoted to helping fellow transgender and gender diverse people. Consider going with the transgender person and getting tested yourself. Having someone to go with can help them over the anxiety of having to do it alone.

What do Transgender and Gender Diverse People Need?

Time to find themselves

People who are attempting to find themselves after being assigned the incorrect gender at birth do not have an easy task. For cisgender people who were assigned the correct gender at birth, who they are in regard to gender is defined for them, even if in broad strokes, by societal standards. It's not to say that cisgender people must live within boundaries, but in many instances, they can just accept societal norms because this make them happy. Transgender and gender diverse people are often challenged to find ways to express themselves that violate social norms and so therefore face opposition and push back from those around them. They need time to explore and accepting people that give them the space to do so.

Access to safe restrooms

The most toxic effect of the bathroom battles is that it makes it hard for people whose gender presentation does not match expectations to exist in public spaces. If you can't use a restroom, how do you eat at the mall or a restaurant or attend a sports event? Many argue discrimination is the real goal of the legislative attempts that want to legislate transgender people out of existence or back into the closet.

To be able to live in safe housing

Most people assume that it is illegal to discriminate with regards to housing, but in most places, it is not. Simply violating gender norms is enough to trigger eviction or be denied a rental contract. Maybe it will be announced or more likely, they will just be denied or evicted with no reason.

Medical insurance that covers their needs

Towards the end of the Obama administration, regulation changes began to cause a dramatic increase in medical coverage of care associated with transition. This halted and went backwards shortly after the Trump Administration took office and reversed regulations. Large companies are often the best places to receive coverage as the insurance pool means adding coverage for the relatively few transgender people who work there adds just a few cents to premiums. Meanwhile, the value to the transitioning person is invaluable in terms of the care they receive as well as the validation of being able to see a doctor for care.

Access to trained medical personnel, if required

Especially in rural areas, it is often hard or impossible to find a sympathetic doctor with the knowledge required to help with care. Add the complexities of finding one on your insurance, even if that specific care is not covered, and it just means that transgender people often cannot get qualified and trained medical personnel surrounding their transition. Planned Parenthood and some others have recently been expanding into this space, but geographic gaps in care cover much of the United States.

Access to legal advice, if required

Navigating the complexities of name and gender marker change are just one area where legal advice is required. Even minor police interactions can turn into a major crisis for transgender people as their ID may not match their gender presentation.

Transgender or gender diverse people are very often openly discriminated against or placed in very dangerous situations when they are boarded with the prison or jail populations corresponding to their gender assigned at birth. Access to hormones needs to be maintained and long-term sentences may require help receiving medical care.

Activists who work with prison populations say that often the best way to improve the lives of incarcerated transgender or gender diverse people is to draw attention to the circumstances at the facility. Seek out activists who work with these populations as the experts needed to make a difference.

Peers and mentors that understand them

Not having access to others like them can feel very isolating and othering. It can wreak havoc on self-esteem. Transphobic statements that have been repeated over and over get compounded by not seeing anyone else like them and manifest in internalized transphobia and self-hate. Simple, even limited, connection to people who share their experiences are incredibly validating. In instances where there is nobody geographically near them, social media can help fill the gap and travel to conventions an incredible boost.

A vision of what their future looks like

Being allowed to focus on the challenges they face daily without having a vision of a successful future can lead to hopelessness. This is a continuation of the peer and mentor discussion.

To be addressed by their chosen name

This seems so simple but is so validating. In contrast, repeatedly having to correct people or ignore the dead naming is a constant reminder you are rejected. While the people using a dead name may think they are trying to convince the transgender person the error of their ways, it only sends the message that the love they receive is conditional.

It's common practice to grant or even assign people nicknames. I went by a nickname for my whole life, yet for some, calling people by a name they chose when it validates their gender identity is too far. It is an attack without blood but not without scars.

To be addressed using the proper pronouns

Just like chosen name, using the proper pronouns is validation. It's an expression of love and acceptance. To not do so is an attack on their very being.

In much of America, everyone is taught to use sir or ma'am when addressing people they don't know. I suggest you use either their name or avoid a gender designation at all. You don't know them and do not know their gender identity. Your attempt to be polite means little to those who you happen to address correctly, but it is a serious affront when you use it incorrectly. This does not only affect people who are transgender or gender diverse, cisgender people also struggle with being addressed incorrectly, and it is just as offensive to them. You don't know. Unlearn this false politeness.

To not be required to teach others about gender

As you can imagine from the section about the coming out process, having to teach everyone they interact with about gender becomes exhausting. For most transgender or gender diverse people, they just want to live their lives. If you run into a gender identity or other term that you do not understand, terms can be looked up on the internet. Choose several different sources to make sure you get the most valid definition and best understanding.   Tumbler has a comprehensive list of gender identities complete with definitions.

Likely legally protected by FERPA/ HIPPAA

If you are an administrator, teacher, or medical professional, realize that their privacy associated with their gender identity is a medical diagnosis. You cannot routinely share or gossip about them.

Social norms – if you wouldn't ask a cis person, don't ask a trans person

In addition to the endless questions about gender and pronoun use , gender diverse and transgender people are constantly asked about the status of their genitals, their hormones, and various other seemingly random questions. Before asking any question, ask yourself how you would feel if that question was asked of you. Then if you believe it is an appropriate question, proceed.

To be able to move through life unencumbered

The sum of these small items is that transgender and gender diverse people just want to live their lives and go about their business with the same level of freedom as everyone else.

Feel welcome in their community

In addition to being able to live their lives unencumbered, feeling welcome and invited into their communities is vital to a happy life. We all seek out community and shared experience. Nobody wants to feel isolated and ostracized. The constant stream of challenges, though, can make them hesitant to make the first step, to introduce themselves, to put themselves out there. Reach out to them and invite them. Bring them with you. Intentionally include them. That is an ally.

Privilege

Repeatedly throughout the book we have talked about privilege and marginalization. That is because this dramatically affects the experience of being a part of the transgender or gender diverse community. Over and over again, in a million different ways, privilege or marginalization build upon each other to dramatically change people's lives.

Invisibility

We talked about this briefly before, but it warrants repeating.

We have all had the feeling of entering a space where we didn't feel like we belonged. Maybe you walked into a room filled with people of a different gender or race and everyone appeared to stop and look at you. You were not invisible.

This is a key difference when we start talking about transgender and gender diverse people. As they transition, many lose the ability to be invisible.

For example, a lesbian or gay couple can pass as heterosexual by avoiding public displays of affection. Something as innocent as holding hands though destroys that invisibility. They may then become the targets of bigotry and discrimination.

If you are a racial minority, you never had that invisibility. Whenever you enter a room, you are more likely than not to stand out. People in the room apply stereotypes gleaned from media and movies and their own racism.

Many transgender people are so afraid of losing that invisibility, they may obsess over passing to the point that they cannot leave their home with their gender expression matching their gender identity. Their fear traps them in the closet.

A good ally will look out for circumstances like this. Invite the person into your group and engage them in the conversation. Make them feel welcome and at home.

Family acceptance

Many transgender and gender diverse people lose the support of their family when they transition. Depending on their age and other circumstances, this can be devastating. It is not hard to find stories of trans people kicked out of their homes at a young age. You can imagine how events like this dramatically change the arc of their lives. Other people who transition after they are established are more insulated to this kind of influences but still suffer the emotional consequences of this withholding of love and support.

Spousal support

Rare is the marriage that floats through one partner's transition without consequence. There are so many factors at play that many marriages do not survive. Transition is, as we know, fraught with no shortage of challenges and having a partner there to lean on can be invaluable, but many of those same challenges may become too much for the non-transitioning spouse. At a minimum, finding an experienced therapist to help navigate the emotions is a good idea.

Employment

Few legal protections exist for transgender and gender diverse people. Even those that exist are often challenging to enforce and prove as employers rarely directly state they are terminating employment because of a transition. Just as an illustration of how privilege builds upon each other, jobs that require specialized training or education are also the same ones that are more likely to be accepting and even affirming of a transition.

Community Support

The support of communities can have a dramatic impact on the lives of its members. This support ranges from emotional support to actual assistance in times of crisis. Many a transitioning person has been quietly excluded from their community or worse, outright publicly condemned. Imagine showing up at church after announcing your transition and having to sit through a sermon condemning transgender people. It happens. In sharp contrast, some churches and organizations go out of their way to be supportive and affirming. They bring in speakers to educate the community and participate in PRIDE marches. Some have supportive and affirming education programs for teens that include discussions of gender identity and sexual orientation.

Race

Few things highlight the disparity in privilege and opportunity more than an examination of the transgender people murdered each year for who they are. With strikingly little deviation, the people murdered are transgender women of color.

Significant Days

Transgender Day of Visibility

March 31st of each year, transgender and gender diverse people make an effort to be visible and to educate. Often on social media, they post offers to answer any well-meaning question. Organizations bring in speakers or show documentaries. At the time of writing, fewer than one third of Americans say they know someone who is transgender. Breaking through the veil of fear created by that invisibility makes people more accepting and empathetic. It tears down the opportunities created by anonymity that are so often exploited by those seeking to marginalize and discriminate.

Transgender Day of Remembrance

November 20th of each year, transgender and gender diverse communities around the U.S. gather to remember and say the names of the transgender and gender diverse people murdered that year for who they are.

Resources

Name and Gender Marker Change

- National Center for Transgender Equality
  https://www.transequality.org/documents
- LAMBDA Legal
  https://www.lambdalegal.org/know-your-rights/article/trans-changing-birth-certificate-sex-designations

General Information

- Human Rights Campaign
  http://www.hrc.org/explore/topic/transgender
- National Center for Transgender Equality
  https://www.transequality.org/
- LAMBDA Legal
  https://www.lambdalegal.org/issues/transgender-rights
- GLAAD
  https://www.glaad.org/transgender/resources
- Trevor Project FAQs
  http://www.thetrevorproject.org/pages/support-center
- Gay, lesbian and straight education network
  http://www.glsen.org

Suicide Prevention Numbers

- Trans Lifeline
  US: (877) 565-8860
  Canada: (877) 330-6366
  https://www.translifeline.org/
- Trevor Project
  866-488-7386
  Chat/Text/Call:
  http://www.thetrevorproject.org/pages/get-help-now

Social Networking
- Dedicated Social Networking Site for LGBTQ Youth
  https://www.trevorspace.org
- The Facebook Transgender Alliance
  https://www.facebook.com/groups/TransAlliance1
- Association of Transgender Professionals
  https://www.facebook.com/groups/AssocTransProfessi
  onals
- Transgender-Genderqueer
  https://www.facebook.com/groups/213396725394276
- Transgender Support
  https://www.facebook.com/groups/bethereforus/

Choosing a College
- Campus Pride Index
  College Rankings for LGBTQ Inclusion
  https://www.campusprideindex.org/

Medical Information
- World Professional Organization of Transgender Health
  http://www.wpath.org
- American Medical Association
  https://www.ama-assn.org/delivering-care/policies-
  lesbian-gay-bisexual-transgender-queer-lgbtq-issues
- American Academy of Pediatrics
  https://www.aap.org/en-us/about-the-aap/aap-press-
  room/pages/AAP-Statement-on-Protecting-
  Transgender-Youth.aspx
  Note: You may find references to the American College
  of Pediatricians but this is a tiny fringe group of
  politically motivated pediatricians.
- American Psychological Association
  http://www.apa.org/topics/lgbt/transgender.aspx

Studies:

Diamond, Milton (May 2013). "Transexuality Among Twins: Identity Concordance,m Transition Rearing, and Orientation". International Journal of Transgenderism. Retrieved 14 June 2015

Swaab, Dick F; Castellanos-Cruz, L; Bao, A. -M "The Human Brain and Gender Sexual Differentiation of Our Brains." In: Schreiber, Gerhard. Transexuality in Theology and Neuroscience. Findings, Controversies, and Perspectives. Berlin and Boston: Walter de Gruyter 2016 (ISBN 978-3-11-044080-5) pp. 23-42

Kruijver, G.P.M.; Zhou, JN; Pool, CW; Hofman, MA; Gooren, LJ; Swaab, DF (2000) "Male to Female Transexuals Have Female Neuron Numbers in a Limbic Nucleus" Journal of Clinical Endocrinology & Metabolism. 85 (5): 2014-41. PMID 10843193 doi:10.1210/jcem.85.5.6564

Kern, Scott "Prenatal DiEthylStilbestrol Exposure in Males and Gender-related Disorders. International Behavioral Development Symposium 2005

Acknowledgements

For volunteering to lend your professional editing skills this effort, I want to send a special thanks to Alisa. You have been a great help.

I also want to thank Lisle Soukup, Beth Buyse and Brandon Beck (https://transteacher.com) who without complaint read drafts of the book and provided me with valuable insight.

Made in the USA
San Bernardino, CA
17 June 2018